With love,
Ei d h

Dec 17, 2010

tuscany

tuscany

a culinary journey of discovery

PAMELA GWYTHER

MARKS &
SPENCER

Marks and Spencer p.l.c.
PO Box 3339
Chester CH99 9QS

shop online
www.marksandspencer.com

ISBN: 978-1-84461-663-3

Printed in China

Produced by the Bridgewater Book Company Ltd

Photography: Laurie Evans
Home economist: Carol Tennant

Notes for the Reader
This book uses both metric and imperial measurements. Follow the same units of measurement throughout; do not mix metric and imperial. All spoon measurements are level: teaspoons are assumed to be 5 ml, and tablespoons are assumed to be 15 ml. Unless otherwise stated, milk is assumed to be full fat, eggs and individual vegetables such as potatoes are medium and pepper is freshly ground black pepper. Recipes using raw or very lightly cooked eggs should be avoided by infants, the elderly, pregnant women, convalescents and anyone suffering from an illness. The times given are an approximate guide only.

Picture Acknowledgements
The publisher would like to thank the following for permission to reproduce copyright material: Owaki – Kulla/Corbis (pages 6 to 11, edges), Desgrieux/PhotoCuisine/Corbis (page 30), Envision/Corbis (page 39), Roulier/Turiot/photocuisine/Corbis (page 46), Linda Lewis/PictureArts/Corbis (page 52), Kevin Black/StockFood Creative/Getty (page 53), Marianna Day Massey/ZUMA/Corbis (page 60), J. Riou/photocuisine/Corbis (page 73), Ed Young/Corbis (page 74), Gregor Schuster/zefa/Corbis (page 75), Photonica /Getty (page 76) and Rita Maas/PictureArts/Corbis (page 86).

Contents

Introduction

Italy has several provinces, each one endowed with individual characteristics and culture derived from its own particular climate, geography and history. The provinces range from the hot, dry areas in the south to the cooler foothills of the Alps in the north. None, though, has as rich and diverse a climate, culture and cuisine as Tuscany.

A little history

The region of Tuscany first came to prominence in the eleventh century BC, as the home of the Etruscan civilization. Later, under the influence of the Romans, it became known as Tuscia. This powerful heritage developed Tuscany into the world's most prominent culture in the second millennium. Michelangelo, Dante, Cellini and Brunelleschi, among other renowned figures, led an artistic and literary revolution, supported by the wealth and power of dynasties such as the Medicis. Florence became the symbol of these riches, although other towns such as Siena, Pisa and Lucca all rose to importance.

Tuscany first gained popularity with the British in the nineteenth century, attracting literary giants such as Shelley, Byron, the Brownings and Tennyson. They were followed in the twentieth century by Virginia Woolf and E M Forster, all of whom found the unique culture and climate a welcome alternative to the cold damp of their homeland.

Tuscan cuisine

It is this temperate climate, coupled with a region abundant in the produce of both soil and sea, that has created the characteristic cuisine of Tuscany. From the green hills topped with poplars and cypresses to the flatter Maremma region in the south comes a rich variety of meat and game, including the ever-popular wild boar. The best beef in Italy comes from the Chiano, south of Arezzo, and the Tyrrhenian Sea provides a fine range of fish for Tuscan fish stews or the lightly fried *Fritto Misto di Mare*.

History has left its mark on Tuscan food, too. For example, Siena's famous panforte cake owes its origins to the spices brought in visiting caravans from the Orient in the Middle Ages. Tomatoes originated from Sicily but were brought to Tuscany by Garibaldi's soldiers in the nineteenth century. The same century saw maize being imported for the first time, which is now a staple food, particularly in the form of polenta.

Classic ingredients

Olive oil

Some Tuscan products are, however, timeless. The region still produces some of the best olive oil in Italy – fragrant, rich, slightly peppery, but full of health-promoting properties. It is low in cholesterol compared to other fats, and rich in vitamin E, so therefore beneficial for the skin. The lower the acidity, the better the oil, and the best comes from around Lucca, although each of Tuscany's ten sub-regions has its own speciality. Extra-virgin olive oil must be below 1 per cent in acidity and is ideal for drizzling on salads or onto bruschetta and over grilled meats and fish. Higher levels of acidity make for a cheaper olive oil, which is best used for frying.

The olive harvest takes place from October to December, when the trees in the olive groves have nets spread under them to catch the ripe fruit as the trees are shaken. But the highest quality and most expensive oils are made from hand-picked fruit to avoid damage to the trees, which can sometimes live for over a century. The fruit is pressed twice to extract the oil – a first light and cold pressing followed by a more forceful squeezing under pressure and at a higher temperature. The first extraction is the most highly prized and priced.

Beans

Another timeless and typical Tuscan staple is the bean. There are many varieties, the oldest being black-eyed beans, which were grown in Roman times. In the fifteenth century, as trading links developed with the recently discovered New World, white or cannellini beans were first imported. They proved highly suitable for the rich Tuscan soil and warm temperate climate. Borlotti beans are also popular, available in shades of red, cream and magenta. Beans constitute a low-cost, high-protein, energy-providing staple ingredient. Their mild flavours and textures go well with strongly flavoured yet simple Tuscan dishes.

Pork and ham

Pork and ham are also key ingredients in their many dried, cured forms. There are two main varieties. *Prosciutto* (which means 'dried') is a thinly sliced, tasty ham that has been preserved through air-drying, and is best eaten with vegetables or fresh Tuscan bread and olive oil. *Salami* (which means 'salted') is also dried but is made from finely cut pork combined with spices, herbs and salt. Both prosciutto and salami should be dried for at least six months before eating. *Pancetta* is another variety, made from belly pork. Sausages are also very popular in the region.

The importance of simplicity…

Tuscan culinary skills have been preserved by generations of cooks and in the many small, family-run restaurants. With such a wide range of premium raw materials available to them, a style has evolved that is based on simplicity, using only the freshest ingredients, in season and of magnificent quality, unadorned with anything to mask their basic excellence. Consequently, the bold, natural flavours come through, undisguised by sauces or cream and butter, and accompanied only perhaps by fresh bread. Cooking methods are kept simple, too. Meat and poultry are generally just roasted or grilled, preferably over an open wood fire. Vegetable dishes are served separately and are often a meal in themselves.

Bread, locally baked or home-made to traditional recipes and generally unsalted so that the flavours of the main dishes are not compromised, is the main accompaniment. For those new to it, *pane sciocco* or *toscano* (Tuscan bread) can be something of a challenge. It is truly bland, but the lack of salt has an interesting history. Salt was an essential economic and medicinal commodity in times gone by. Indeed, many English words have their roots in the Latin word for salt, *sal*. 'Salary', for example, derives from the Latin *salarium argentums* or salt money. In the sixteenth century, the Papacy tried to impose a salt tax on the fiercely independent Tuscans, who retaliated by refusing to put salt in their bread. Having done so, they discovered how well it helped maintain the flavours of the wonderful raw materials in the rest of the meal, so have continued the habit to this day. However, the bread is not completely without flavour – the unique taste of the natural yeasts and the artisan flours captured in hand-made breads cooked in wood-fired ovens can be captivating. The main shapes are the round *bozza*, the long *filone* and the more familiar *ciabatta*. Sometimes, flavours are added in the form of nuts, olives, onions or spices.

...and the seasons

A Tuscan cook typically has to provide two full meals a day for his or her family, which is another major reason why a simple approach to meal planning has evolved. It is made easier by the habit of daily shopping in local markets that are full of the fresh produce of the season. Tuscan cooks would not dream of buying and eating fruit or vegetables, meat or fish outside their natural seasons. And why should they, when each season brings an abundance of gloriously fresh colours, textures and flavours?

The countryside begins to awaken in the spring, when markets fill with fresh young vegetables and salads, including tender broad beans that can be eaten raw. Both wild and white asparagus varieties appear, along with a whole range of artichokes – small and large, green and blue. Green or 'wet' garlic (garlic that is fresh from the ground) and spring onions, early rosemary and sage all add their particular flavour to salads and meats.

Summer sees Tuscany's most prolific natural bounty piled high in the markets. Tomatoes offer different shapes, sizes and colours for salads or for preserving or making into a sauce or paste. Courgettes, peppers and aubergines add vibrant colour to the market as well as variety to the plate. Carrots, onions and celery cry out to be chopped and simmered in fragrant olive oil. Fine green beans are followed by fresh cannellini beans and then by the colourful borlotti beans. Aromatic basil, parsley, oregano and marjoram are just waiting to enhance all manner of delicious dishes.

Summer is also the prime time for fruit. Sweet cherries and strawberries start the season, followed by apricots, peaches and nectarines as the temperature rises. As the heat increases further, different varieties of melon come to the fore – fragrant cantaloupe varieties for eating with prosciutto, and bigger and juicier watermelons to quench the thirst. Fresh figs and dessert grapes, along with almonds, are served to end the meal.

The coming of autumn signals another change in eating. Mushrooms in a range of varieties – porcini being the most popular – appear and are used to add additional flavour to stews, to add interest to salads and omelettes or for simply grilling with olive oil. It is also the time for truffles. White or black, they are highly prized and hugely expensive yet wonderfully flavoursome and can turn a simple risotto or pasta dish into an extravagant feast. Pumpkins are roasted, made into soups or used to stuff ravioli. Apples and pears of all shapes and flavours abound and are frequently eaten with pecorino cheese and fresh walnuts.

Autumn, too, is the time of the grape harvest. Tuscan wines are as good as the food they accompany so well. Quaffable whites are made from the trebbiano and vernaccia grapes, and are ideal chilled as an aperitif or served with grilled fish. Delightful reds, using the sangiovese grape, are equally palatable with pasta and meat dishes. Particularly famous is Chianti, with the best *classico* coming from the area between Florence and Siena, although even better quality red wine can be found in Montepulciano and Montalcino. A local speciality wine – Vin Santo – embodies all that is best in Tuscan cuisine. It is a sweet wine made from grapes hung in smoky kitchens to concentrate the flavours, and is generally drunk at the end of a meal to round off a magnificent dining experience.

Now that you have discovered a little more about Tuscan cooking, you can look forward to preparing, cooking and enjoying for yourself the many culinary delights that Tuscany has to offer by sampling the full range of recipes that follows.

Starters
and Soups

Antipasti are appetizers and, as the name suggests, the dishes that come before the pasta course. A typical selection could include cold meats or vegetables simply served with a little extra-virgin olive oil.

Antipasti can be either hot or cold depending on the season. Hot dishes could include a grilled slice of bread with a topping. Cold dishes generally are similar to salads, with a vegetable base enhanced by olive oil.

There are three main types of soup. Plain broths are popular, although thicker soups are favoured in cooler weather. Best of all, though, are the really thick varieties, heavy with beans and other pulses or vegetables.

Wild mushroom bruschetta

Bruschetta di funghi

Serves 4

4 slices sourdough bread, such as Pugliese

3 garlic cloves, 1 halved and 2 crushed

2 tbsp extra-virgin olive oil

225 g/8 oz mixed wild mushrooms, such as porcini, chanterelles and field mushrooms

1 tbsp olive oil

25 g/1 oz butter

1 small onion or 2 shallots, finely chopped

50 ml/2 fl oz dry white wine or Marsala

salt and pepper

2 tbsp roughly chopped fresh flat-leaf parsley, to garnish

Bruschetta, like crostini, are grilled or griddled slices of country bread that are rubbed with garlic and drizzled with the very best extra-virgin olive oil. A variety of toppings can then be added, such as this mushroom one.

Toast the bread slices under a preheated grill or in a preheated ridged griddle pan on both sides, rub with the garlic halves and drizzle with the extra-virgin olive oil. Transfer to a baking sheet and keep warm in a warm oven.

Wipe the mushrooms thoroughly to remove any trace of soil and slice any large ones. Heat the olive oil with half the butter in a frying pan, add the mushrooms and cook over a medium heat, stirring frequently, for 3–4 minutes until soft. Remove with a slotted spoon and keep warm in the oven.

Heat the remaining butter in the frying pan, add the onion and crushed garlic and cook over a medium heat, stirring frequently, for 3–4 minutes until soft. Add the wine, stir well and leave to bubble for 2–3 minutes until reduced and thickened. Return the mushrooms to the frying pan and heat through. The sauce should be thick enough to glaze the mushrooms. Season to taste with salt and pepper.

Pile the mushrooms on top of the warm bruschetta, scatter with the parsley and serve immediately.

Bread and tomato soup

Pappa al pomodoro

Serves 6

450 g/1 lb two-day-old crusty Italian open-textured bread, such as Pugliese

1 kg/2 lb 4 oz ripe plum tomatoes

4 tbsp olive oil

4 garlic cloves, crushed

500 ml/18 fl oz boiling water

1 bunch of fresh basil

salt and pepper

6 tbsp extra-virgin olive oil, to serve

The simplest of Tuscan soups that relies on really fresh ingredients, this is best made at the height of the summer when the tomatoes are at their sweetest and the basil is at its most fragrant.

Cut the bread into slices and then cubes (you can remove some of the crusts if you wish) and leave to dry out for 30 minutes. Meanwhile, peel the tomatoes (see Cook's Tip) and cut into chunks.

Heat the olive oil in a large saucepan, add the garlic and cook over a medium heat, stirring, for 1 minute without browning. Add the tomatoes and simmer gently for 20–30 minutes until the mixture has thickened.

Add the bread and stir until it has absorbed the liquid. Stir in the boiling water until you have a thick soupy mixture. Season well with salt and pepper (salt quantities will vary according to the type of bread used).

Remove the basil leaves from their stems and tear any large leaves into pieces. Stir the basil into the soup.

Serve warm with a tablespoonful of extra-virgin olive oil sprinkled over each bowl.

Cook's tip
Peel the tomatoes by plunging them into a heatproof bowl of boiling water for 10–15 seconds, then transfer with a slotted spoon to a bowl of cold water. Pierce the skins with a sharp knife and, when cool enough to handle, peel away the skins.

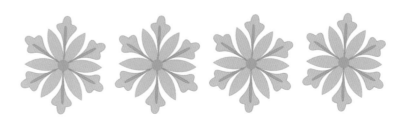

Traditional bean and cabbage soup

Ribollita

Serves 6

200 g/7 oz dried cannellini beans, soaked in cold water overnight

3 tbsp olive oil

2 red onions, roughly chopped

4 carrots, peeled and sliced

4 celery sticks, roughly chopped

4 garlic cloves, roughly chopped

600 ml/1 pint water or vegetable stock

400 g/14 oz canned chopped tomatoes

2 tbsp chopped fresh flat-leaf parsley

500 g/1 lb 2 oz cavolo nero, trimmed and finely sliced

1 small two-day-old ciabatta loaf, torn into small pieces

salt and pepper

extra-virgin olive oil, to serve

This is a traditional peasant Tuscan soup and is very robust. Cavolo nero is now widely available, but if necessary you could use a dark Savoy cabbage.

Drain the beans and put in a large saucepan. Cover with fresh cold water and bring to the boil, skimming off any scum that rises to the surface with a slotted spoon. Reduce the heat and simmer, uncovered, for 1–1½ hours until tender, topping up with water if required.

Meanwhile, heat the olive oil in a large saucepan, add the onions, carrots and celery and cook over a medium heat, stirring frequently, for 10–15 minutes until softened. Add the garlic and cook, stirring, for 1–2 minutes.

Drain the beans, reserving the cooking water, and add half the beans to the vegetable mixture. Pour in the measured water and tomatoes, add the parsley and season well with salt and pepper. Bring to a simmer and cook, uncovered and stirring occasionally, for 30 minutes. Add the cavolo nero and cook, stirring occasionally, for a further 15 minutes.

Put the remaining beans in a food processor or blender with some of the reserved cooking water and process until smooth. Add to the soup. Stir in the bread. The soup should be thick, but add more of the reserved cooking water to thin if necessary. Continue to cook until heated through.

Serve hot with a drizzle of extra-virgin olive oil.

Cook's tip

You can use 400 g/14 oz canned cannellini beans instead of the dried beans to save time. Drain and process in a food processor or blender with a little stock or water until smooth.

Chickpea soup

Zuppa di ceci

Serves 6

400 g/14 oz dried chickpeas, soaked in cold water overnight

2 tbsp olive oil

1 onion, finely chopped

2 garlic cloves, finely chopped

450 g/1 lb Swiss chard, trimmed and finely sliced

2 fresh rosemary sprigs

400 g/14 oz canned chopped tomatoes

salt and pepper

slices of toasted bread, to serve

Chickpeas are another Tuscan staple, used in soups, stews and vegetable dishes. They become stale very quickly, so check the 'use by' date on the packet.

Drain the chickpeas and put in a large saucepan. Cover with fresh cold water and bring to the boil, skimming off any scum that rises to the surface with a slotted spoon. Reduce the heat and simmer, uncovered, for 1–1¼ hours until tender, topping up with water if necessary.

Drain the chickpeas, reserving the cooking water. Season the chickpeas well with salt and pepper. Put two-thirds in a food processor or blender with some of the reserved cooking water and process until smooth, adding more of the cooking water if necessary to give a soup consistency. Return to the saucepan.

Heat the oil in a medium saucepan, add the onion and garlic and cook over a medium heat, stirring frequently, for 3–4 minutes until the onion has softened. Add the Swiss chard and rosemary sprigs and cook, stirring frequently, for 3–4 minutes. Add the tomatoes and cook for a further 5 minutes, or until the tomatoes have broken down to an almost smooth sauce. Remove the rosemary sprigs.

Add the Swiss chard and tomato mixture to the chickpea purée and simmer for 2–3 minutes. Taste and adjust the seasoning if necessary.

Serve in warmed bowls with warm slices of toasted bread on the side.

Chestnut and pancetta soup

Minestra di castagne e pancetta

Serves 4–6

3 tbsp olive oil

175 g/6 oz pancetta, cut into strips

2 onions, finely chopped

2 carrots, peeled and finely chopped

2 celery sticks, finely chopped

350 g/12 oz dried chestnuts, soaked in cold water overnight

2 garlic cloves, finely chopped

1 tbsp finely chopped fresh rosemary

1 litre/1¾ pints good-quality chicken stock

salt and pepper

extra-virgin olive oil, to serve

Sweet chestnuts are gathered in October in the Chianti region of Tuscany. Dried chestnuts or the vacuum-packed variety make this recipe simple to make at home.

Heat the olive oil in a large saucepan, add the pancetta and cook over a medium heat, stirring frequently, for 2–3 minutes until starting to brown.

Add the onions, carrots and celery and cook, stirring frequently, for 10 minutes, or until slightly golden and softened.

Drain the chestnuts, add to the saucepan with the garlic and rosemary and stir well. Pour in the stock, bring to a simmer and cook, uncovered, for 30–35 minutes until the chestnuts are beginning to soften and break down – this thickens the soup.

Season well with salt and pepper and serve immediately in warmed deep dishes with the extra-virgin olive oil drizzled over.

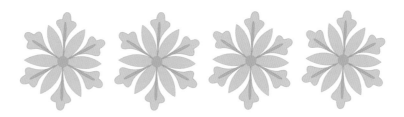

Tuscan summer salad

Panzanella

Serves 4

8 large ripe tomatoes

2 garlic cloves, crushed

6 tbsp extra-virgin olive oil, plus extra to serve

2 tbsp red wine vinegar or balsamic vinegar

225 g/8 oz two-day-old Tuscan saltless bread or other rustic country bread

1 red onion, halved through the root and cut into fine crescent shapes

small handful of fresh basil leaves, coarsely torn into pieces

salt and pepper

This is a traditional simple bread and tomato salad. If you have not made any Tuscan saltless bread, use another rustic country bread such as ciabatta.

Halve the tomatoes and remove and discard the seeds, then cut the flesh into eighths. Put in a sieve over a bowl to collect the juice.

Add the garlic to the tomato juice and season well with salt and pepper. Pour in the oil and vinegar and stir well.

Break the bread up into rough pieces and put in a large bowl. Pour over the tomato juice mixture and gently stir until the bread has absorbed all the juice. Rub the bread between your fingers to break it into smaller pieces, handling it very carefully to avoid breaking it up too much.

Place a layer of the soaked bread in a serving dish and spoon over half the tomatoes and onion. Add another layer of bread and top with the remaining tomatoes, onion and the basil. Cover and leave to stand at room temperature for 1 hour for the flavours to be absorbed by the bread.

Stir well, taste and adjust the seasoning if necessary and drizzle with a little extra oil before serving.

Cook's tip
You can add grilled peppers, capers, anchovies and olives to this salad, but the simple recipe is more traditional.

Ham and salami salad with figs

Insalata di prosciutto, salami e fichi

Serves 6

9–12 ripe figs, depending on size

6 thin slices dry-cured Italian ham

12 thin slices salami

1 small bunch of fresh basil, separated into small sprigs

few fresh mint sprigs

1 small bunch of rocket leaves

2 tbsp freshly squeezed lemon juice

4 tbsp extra-virgin olive oil

salt and pepper

Figs are an integral part of Italian food, not only as a dessert but served, as here, as a starter with cured ham and salami. Make sure that the figs are ripe and soft, as unripe figs are disappointingly lacking in flavour.

Trim the stems of the figs to leave just a short length, then cut the figs into quarters.

Arrange the ham and salami on a large serving platter.

Wash and dry the herbs and rocket and put in a bowl with the prepared figs.

Whisk the lemon juice and oil together with a fork in a small bowl and season well with salt and pepper. Pour over the herbs and salad leaves and carefully turn the figs and leaves in the dressing until they are well coated.

Spoon the figs and salad onto the meat and arrange around the platter.

Artichoke and asparagus salad

Insalata di carciofi e asparagi

Serves 6

6 small globe artichokes

juice of 1 lemon

225 g/8 oz fine asparagus spears

6 tbsp extra-virgin olive oil

70 g/2½ oz pitted black olives

3 anchovy fillets in oil, drained and chopped

2 tbsp chopped fresh flat-leaf parsley

salt and pepper

85 g/3 oz Parmesan cheese, shaved

Artichokes and asparagus are wonderful summer vegetables and are only in season for a short time. Make sure you buy them as fresh as possible to enjoy simply with olive oil or melted butter, or, as here, in a salad.

Trim the stems of the artichokes to 1 cm/ ½ inch in length and cut off the top quarter of the leaves. Bring a large saucepan of water with half the lemon juice added to the boil and add the artichokes. Reduce the heat and simmer for 15–20 minutes until the leaves pull away easily.

Meanwhile, cut off the woody ends of the asparagus and if necessary shave some of the fibrous stalk away. Wipe thoroughly and cook in an asparagus cooker (a tall saucepan that allows the stems to be cooked upright so that the tips are steamed) or simmer in a large frying pan until tender. This should take 5–8 minutes. Drain and leave to cool, then season well with salt and pepper and drizzle with half the oil.

Drain the artichokes, then cool under cold running water and turn upside down to drain. Peel away the tough outside leaves of the artichokes to leave only the tender leaves. Using a sharp knife, cut each artichoke into quarters and remove the hairy choke. Put in a bowl, season well with salt and pepper and add a drizzle of the remaining oil.

Arrange the artichokes and asparagus on individual serving plates and scatter over the olives, anchovies and parsley. Drizzle over the remaining lemon juice and oil and top with the Parmesan cheese shavings before serving.

Cook's tip
If you don't have the time or inclination to prepare fresh artichokes, buy small artichoke hearts in a jar or in cans, drain them and halve – you will need 12.

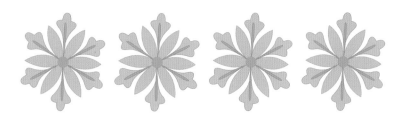

Broad bean and pecorino salad

Insalata di baccelli e pecorino

Serves 6

225 g/8 oz shelled fresh
broad beans

5 tbsp extra-virgin olive oil

2 tbsp freshly squeezed lemon juice

1 tbsp chopped fresh mint

175 g/6 oz young unaged pecorino
cheese, cut into cubes

90 g/3¼ oz rocket leaves

55 g/2 oz aged pecorino or
Parmesan cheese, shaved

salt and pepper

This salad is designed to be enjoyed in May/June when fresh broad beans are at their most tender. If your broad beans are not so young, you will need to remove the outer skins.

If the beans are extremely fresh and tiny, you can serve them raw, but otherwise blanch them for 2–3 minutes in a large saucepan of boiling water. Drain, rinse under cold running water and drain again.

Put the drained beans in a dish, pour over the oil and lemon juice and add the mint. Season well with salt and pepper and mix in the pecorino cheese cubes.

Arrange the rocket leaves on a serving dish and spoon over the bean and cheese mixture. Scatter over the cheese shavings and serve.

Cook's tip
If you use older beans or frozen ones, you will need 50 per cent more beans to allow for the removal of the skins. This gives the salad a really lovely bright green colour.

First Courses

Basic bread in Tuscany is ideally home-baked or produced by a local baker using traditional wood-fired ovens. The loaves are a variety of shapes and types. Tuscan pizzas are thin and the toppings simple.

Pasta is, of course, the staple food of Italy. Two tasty Tuscan examples are included here. Gnocchi is another form of pasta-like food. It can be made from semolina or from potatoes and cooked in the same way. A lighter, vegetable gnocchi is also popular in Tuscany.

Risotto is a rich and delicious dish. It should be made with either arborio or carnaroli rice to produce a creamy texture without losing its bite.

Small Tuscan pizzas

Schiacciate

These are small, very thin pizzas that can be served as an antipasto or cut into small slices to serve with an aperitif.

Makes 4

225 g/8 oz strong white flour, plus extra for dusting

2 tsp easy-blend dried yeast

½ tsp salt

1 tbsp olive oil, plus extra for oiling

175 ml/6 fl oz warm water

fresh basil sprigs, to garnish

Topping

140 g/5 oz mozzarella cheese, very thinly sliced

4 slices Italian dry-cured ham, torn into strips

4 ripe plum tomatoes, very finely sliced

salt and pepper

2 tbsp extra-virgin olive oil

Mix the flour, yeast and salt together in a mixing bowl. Make a well in the centre. Mix the olive oil and water together in a jug and pour into the well. Gradually mix the liquid into the flour mixture with a round-bladed knife. Gather the mixture together with your hands to form a soft dough.

Turn the dough out onto a lightly floured work surface and knead for 5–7 minutes until very smooth and elastic. Return the dough to the bowl, cover with a clean tea towel or oiled clingfilm and leave to rise in a warm place for 1 hour, or until doubled in size. Turn out and gently knead again for 1 minute until smooth.

Preheat the oven to 220°C/425°F/Gas Mark 7. Oil 2 baking sheets. Divide the dough into 4 pieces and roll each one into a very thin round. Transfer 2 pizza bases to each prepared baking sheet. Arrange the mozzarella slices on top and then the ham. Top with the tomato slices, season well with salt and pepper and drizzle with the extra-virgin olive oil. Leave to stand in a warm place for 10 minutes, or until slightly risen.

Bake in the preheated oven for 15–20 minutes until golden and crisp. Serve hot, garnished with basil sprigs.

Tuscan saltless bread

Pane toscano

Makes 1 large or 2 smaller loaves

450 g/1 lb strong white flour, plus extra for dusting

1½ tsp easy-blend dried yeast

2 tbsp olive oil, plus extra for oiling

300 ml/10 fl oz warm water

The Tuscans like to eat salty, spicy food such as sausages. This traditional saltless bread is an ideal accompaniment to their highly seasoned food.

Mix the flour and yeast together in a mixing bowl. Make a well in the centre. Mix the olive oil and water together in a jug and pour into the well. Gradually mix the liquid into the flour mixture with a round-bladed knife. Gather the mixture together with your hands to form a soft dough.

Turn the dough out onto a lightly floured work surface and knead for 5–7 minutes until very smooth and elastic. Return the dough to the bowl, cover with a clean tea towel or oiled clingfilm and leave to rise in a warm place for 1 hour, or until doubled in size. Turn out and gently knead again for 1 minute until smooth.

Preheat the oven to 200°C/400°F/Gas Mark 6. Oil 1–2 baking sheets. Shape the dough into 1 large oval or 2 smaller ovals and transfer to the prepared baking sheet or sheets. Cover with a clean tea towel or oiled clingfilm and leave to rise in a warm place for 30 minutes.

Make several slashes in the top of the bread with a sharp knife. Bake in the preheated oven for 30–35 minutes (or 20–25 minutes for 2 loaves). If the bread is getting too brown, reduce the temperature a little. To test that the bread is cooked, turn it over and tap it on the bottom – it should sound hollow. Leave to cool on a cooling rack.

Flatbread with onion and rosemary

Focaccia con cipolle e rosemarino

Focaccia is a very popular flatbread made all over the region. It can be made simply with olive oil or with added flavourings, as here.

Mix the flour, yeast and salt together in a mixing bowl, then stir in the chopped rosemary. Make a well in the centre. Mix 3 tablespoons of the oil and water together in a jug and pour into the well. Gradually mix the liquid into the flour mixture with a round-bladed knife. Gather the mixture together with your hands to form a soft dough.

Turn the dough out onto a lightly floured work surface and knead for 8–10 minutes until very smooth and elastic. Return the dough to the bowl, cover with a clean tea towel or oiled clingfilm and leave to rise in a warm place for ¾–1 hour, or until doubled in size. Turn out and gently knead again for 1 minute until smooth.

Preheat the oven to 200°C/400°F/Gas Mark 6. Oil a baking sheet. Gently roll the dough out to a round about 30 cm/12 inches in diameter – it doesn't have to be a perfect circle; a slightly oval shape is traditional. Transfer to the prepared baking sheet, cover with a clean tea towel or oiled clingfilm and leave to rise in a warm place for 20–30 minutes.

Make holes about 5 cm/2 inches apart all over the surface of the dough with the handle of a wooden spoon. Spread the onion rings over the dough, drizzle with the remaining oil and scatter over the salt. Bake in the preheated oven for 20–25 minutes until well risen and golden brown. Five minutes before the end of the cooking time, garnish with the rosemary sprigs. Transfer to a wire rack to cool for a few minutes, then serve the bread warm.

Cook's tip
Sun-dried tomatoes and chopped olives can be added before the final rising or just scattered on top for extra flavour.

Flat noodles with aubergines and peppers

Pappardelle con melanzane e peperoni

2 tbsp olive oil

1 red onion, roughly chopped

2 garlic cloves, roughly chopped

55 g/2 oz pancetta, cut into
1-cm/1/2-inch pieces

1 large aubergine, cut into
1-cm/1/2-inch cubes

2 red peppers, deseeded and cut
into strips

125 ml/4 fl oz red wine

400 g/14 oz canned chopped
tomatoes

1 tbsp tomato purée

1 small bunch of fresh basil,
shredded

350 g/12 oz fresh pappardelle

salt and pepper

4 tbsp freshly grated Parmesan
cheese, to serve

Pappardelle with hare (*Pappardelle alla lepre*) is a very traditional Tuscan dish, but given that hare is not easily available, this recipe features the same large ribbon pasta with a rich, thick vegetable sauce.

Heat the oil in a large saucepan, add the onion and garlic and cook over a medium heat, stirring frequently, for 3–4 minutes until starting to soften. Add the pancetta and cook, stirring, for 2–3 minutes until starting to brown. Add the aubergine and red peppers, stir well and cook, stirring occasionally, for 8–10 minutes until softened.

Add the wine, tomatoes and tomato purée and bring to the boil, then reduce the heat and simmer, uncovered, for 4–5 minutes, or until the sauce has thickened and reduced. Season well with salt and pepper and add the basil.

Meanwhile, bring a large saucepan of water to the boil. Add the pappardelle and stir well, return to the boil and cook for 2–3 minutes until al dente or just tender but still firm to the bite. Drain and return to the saucepan, reserving a little of the cooking water.

Pour the sauce into the pasta and stir well, adding the reserved cooking water if necessary – the sauce should be thick but moist.

Serve in warmed dishes with Parmesan cheese to taste.

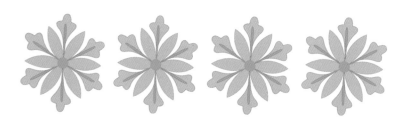

Penne with sausage sauce

Penne con sugo di salsiccie

Serves 4–6

2 tbsp olive oil

1 red onion, roughly chopped

2 garlic cloves, roughly chopped

6 Italian sausages, skinned and the meat crumbled

1/2 tsp dried chilli flakes

2 tbsp chopped fresh oregano

400 g/14 oz canned chopped tomatoes

350 g/12 oz dried penne

salt and pepper

2 tbsp chopped fresh flat-leaf parsley, to garnish

3 tbsp freshly grated Parmesan cheese, to serve

Italian sausages are now widely available, as their spicy flavour is well liked. However, if you can't find them, use good-quality pork sausages instead.

Heat the oil in a large saucepan, add the onion and cook over a medium heat, stirring frequently, for 6–8 minutes until starting to brown. Add the garlic and the crumbled sausages and cook for 8–10 minutes, breaking up the sausages with a wooden spoon.

Add the chilli flakes and oregano and stir well. Pour in the tomatoes and bring to the boil, then reduce the heat and simmer, uncovered, for 4–5 minutes until reduced and thickened. Season to taste with salt and pepper.

Meanwhile, bring a large saucepan of salted water to the boil. Add the penne and stir well, return to the boil and cook for 10–12 minutes, or according to the packet instructions, until al dente or just tender but still firm to the bite. Drain well and return to the saucepan.

Pour the sauce into the pasta and stir well.

Serve in warmed dishes, scattered with the parsley and Parmesan cheese to taste.

Potato gnocchi with walnut pesto

Topini con pesto alla noce

Serves 4

450 g/1 lb floury potatoes

55 g/2 oz Parmesan cheese, freshly grated

1 egg, beaten

200 g/7 oz plain flour, plus extra for dusting

salt and pepper

Pesto

40 g/1½ oz fresh flat-leaf parsley

2 tbsp capers, rinsed

2 garlic cloves

175 ml/6 fl oz extra-virgin olive oil

70 g/2½ oz walnut halves

40 g/1½ oz pecorino or Parmesan cheese, freshly grated

Potato gnocchi must be made with floury potatoes or the gnocchi will be sticky and chewy. In order to have very dry potatoes, it is important to cook the potatoes in their skins.

Boil the potatoes in their skins in a large saucepan of water for 30–35 minutes until tender. Drain well and leave to cool slightly.

Meanwhile, to make the pesto, chop the parsley, capers and garlic, then put in a mortar with the oil, walnuts and salt and pepper to taste. Pound with a pestle to a coarse paste. Add the pecorino cheese and stir well.

When the potatoes are cool enough to handle, peel the skins from the potatoes and pass the flesh through a sieve into a large bowl or press through a potato ricer. While still hot, season well with salt and pepper and add the Parmesan cheese. Beat in the egg and sift in the flour. Lightly mix together, then turn out onto a lightly floured work surface. Knead lightly until the mixture becomes a smooth dough. If it is too sticky, add a little more flour.

Roll the dough out on a lightly floured work surface with your hands into a long log. Cut into 2.5-cm/1-inch pieces and gently press with a fork to give the traditional ridged effect. Transfer to a floured baking sheet and cover with a clean tea towel while you make the remaining gnocchi.

Bring a large saucepan of water to the boil, add the gnocchi, in small batches, and cook for 1–2 minutes. Remove with a slotted spoon and transfer to a warmed serving dish to keep warm while you cook the remaining gnocchi.

Serve the gnocchi in warmed serving bowls with a good spoonful of the pesto on top.

Spinach and ricotta gnocchi

Gnocchi di spinaci e ricotta

Serves 4–6

1 tbsp olive oil

500 g/1 lb 2 oz spinach leaves

225 g/8 oz ricotta cheese

115 g/4 oz Parmesan or pecorino cheese, freshly grated

2 eggs, lightly beaten

55 g/2 oz plain flour, plus extra for dusting

freshly grated nutmeg

salt and pepper

Sauce

2 tbsp olive oil

2 shallots, finely chopped

1 carrot, peeled and finely diced

2 garlic cloves, crushed

800 g/1 lb 12 oz canned chopped tomatoes

1 tbsp tomato purée

6 fresh basil leaves, roughly torn into pieces, plus extra whole fresh basil leaves to garnish

This gnocchi is very different to the previous potato recipe. It is very much lighter and healthier because it is made with eggs, cheese and spinach.

Heat the oil in a large saucepan. Add the spinach and cook, covered, for 1–2 minutes until just wilted. Drain through a sieve and leave to cool, then squeeze out as much water as possible with your hands (you can squeeze it in a clean tea towel to ensure that it is very dry).

Finely chop the spinach and put in a bowl. Add the ricotta cheese, half the Parmesan cheese, the eggs and flour and mix well. Season to taste with salt and pepper and add a good grating of nutmeg. Cover and chill in the refrigerator for at least 1 hour.

Meanwhile, make the sauce. Heat the oil in a saucepan, add the shallots, carrot and garlic and cook over a medium heat, stirring frequently, for 3–4 minutes until softened. Add the tomatoes and tomato purée and bring to the boil, then reduce the heat and simmer, uncovered, for 10–15 minutes until the sauce is reduced and thickened. Season to taste with salt and pepper and add the basil leaves. If you like a smooth sauce, pass it through a sieve or process in a food processor or blender.

To shape the gnocchi, flour a plate and your hands thoroughly. Put a dessertspoonful of the spinach mixture into the palm of one hand, roll gently into an egg shape and transfer to a floured baking sheet. Repeat with the remaining spinach mixture.

Bring a large saucepan of water to a simmer, carefully add the gnocchi, in small batches, and cook gently for 2–3 minutes until they rise to the surface. Remove with a slotted spoon and transfer to a warmed serving dish to keep warm while you cook the remaining gnocchi.

Serve the gnocchi in warmed dishes with the sauce poured over the top, garnished with basil leaves and with Parmesan cheese to taste.

Mushroom risotto

Risotto con funghi

Serves 4

55 g/2 oz dried wild mushrooms

250 ml/9 fl oz warm water

6 tbsp olive oil

280 g/10 oz mixed fresh wild or field mushrooms, thickly sliced

2 garlic cloves, finely chopped

1 tbsp finely chopped fresh thyme

1 onion, finely chopped

350 g/12 oz risotto rice (arborio or carnaroli)

150 ml/5 fl oz dry white wine

700 ml/1¼ pints hot chicken stock

55 g/2 oz butter

115 g/4 oz Parmesan cheese, freshly grated

salt and pepper

2 tbsp finely chopped fresh flat-leaf parsley, to garnish

Mushroom risotto is best made with fresh wild mushrooms when they are in season, but the addition of dried mushrooms to fresh cultivated mushrooms can add a wonderful flavour.

Soak the dried mushrooms in the warm water in a small bowl for 10–15 minutes. Drain, reserving the soaking liquid (sieve it thoroughly to remove any grit). Finely slice the drained mushrooms.

Heat half the oil in a large frying pan, add the fresh mushrooms and cook over a low heat, stirring occasionally, for 10–15 minutes until soft. Add the dried mushrooms and garlic and cook, stirring frequently, for a further 2–3 minutes. Add the thyme and salt and pepper to taste, then remove the mushroom mixture from the frying pan and keep warm.

Heat the remaining oil in the frying pan, add the onion and cook over a low heat, stirring occasionally, for 10–12 minutes until soft. Gently stir in the rice and cook, stirring, for 1 minute. Pour in the wine and cook, stirring, until it has all been absorbed. Add the reserved soaking liquid and cook, stirring, until it has all been absorbed.

Keeping the stock at simmering point in a saucepan, add one ladleful to the rice and cook, stirring constantly, until it has all been absorbed before adding the next ladleful. Continue adding the stock in the same way, stirring well to ensure that the rice does not stick to the frying pan, until it has all been absorbed – this should take 15–20 minutes. The rice should be very creamy in texture, though it should also be al dente or tender but still firm to the bite. Season to taste with salt and pepper.

Remove from the heat and gently stir in the mushroom mixture, butter and half the Parmesan cheese.

Serve immediately on warmed plates, scattered with the parsley and with Parmesan cheese to taste.

Polenta with chargrilled vegetables

Polenta con verdura mista griglia

Serves 4

Polenta

1 litre/1³/₄ pints water

1 tsp salt

250 g/9 oz quick-cook polenta

2 garlic cloves, crushed

¹/₂ tsp dried oregano

2 tbsp freshly grated Parmesan cheese

3 tbsp olive oil

salt and pepper

Chargrilled vegetables

1 red pepper, deseeded and quartered

1 yellow pepper, deseeded and quartered

2 red onions, sliced into thick rings

2 courgettes, sliced lengthways into 3–4 pieces

1 small aubergine, sliced across into 8 pieces

3 tbsp olive oil

1 lemon, halved

2 tbsp chopped fresh mixed herbs, such as flat-leaf parsley, rosemary and thyme, to garnish

Polenta can be served soft, like mashed potato, to accompany meat and fish. It can also be prepared in a thicker form, as here, which is then grilled and served with a variety of toppings.

Bring the water to the boil in a saucepan and add the salt. Pour in the polenta, in a steady stream, stirring constantly. Reduce the heat to low and cook, stirring, for 1 minute, or according to the packet instructions. Beat in the garlic, oregano and Parmesan cheese and season well with salt and pepper.

Use 2 teaspoons of the oil to grease a baking sheet and spoon on the polenta mixture. Spread evenly into a 25-cm/10-inch round, smooth the surface and leave to cool for about 1 hour.

Cut the polenta into 8 wedges and brush with the remaining oil. Cook under a preheated medium–high grill or in a preheated ridged griddle pan over a medium–high heat for 1–2 minutes on each side until golden. Remove and keep warm.

Heat a ridged griddle pan until hot. Brush all the vegetables thoroughly with the oil, add to the griddle pan, in batches, and cook over a medium–high heat for 4–6 minutes, turning occasionally, until marked with golden brown stripes and tender. Remove with a slotted spoon, transfer to a warmed serving dish and keep warm while you cook the remaining vegetables. Squeeze the lemon halves over the vegetables and season well with salt and pepper.

Serve 2 slices of the polenta per person with the chargrilled vegetables on top, scattered with the herbs to garnish.

Cook's tip

A little extra-virgin olive oil can be drizzled over the dish before serving.

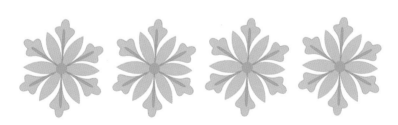

Second Courses

Tuscany is rich in a wide selection of meats, including wild boar, game birds and hare and rabbit. Lamb is also popular, and pigs provide pork, sausages and dried meats. The coastal regions are rich in varieties of fish and shellfish, and inland there are also good freshwater fish.

Chickens are kept both for their eggs and for their flesh. Portions of chicken are often wrapped in pancetta or ham to protect the fragile meat.

Vegetables are an important part of the diet and a huge variety is available all year round. Side dishes of vegetables can be a meal in themselves, particularly with the addition of cheese or dried meats.

Livorno seafood stew

Il cacciucco alla Livornese

Serves 6

4 red mullet fillets

450 g/1 lb monkfish tail

400 g/14 oz cleaned baby squid

3 tbsp olive oil

1 onion, finely chopped

2 garlic cloves, finely chopped

2 fennel bulbs, finely sliced

150 ml/5 fl oz dry white wine

600 g/1 lb 5 oz canned chopped tomatoes

500 g/1 lb 2 oz live mussels, scrubbed and debearded

700 ml/1¼ pints fish stock

18 large raw prawns, peeled and deveined

salt and pepper

To serve

6 slices ciabatta bread, toasted, rubbed with garlic and drizzled with olive oil

2 tbsp finely chopped fresh flat-leaf parsley

This fish stew usually contains at least five varieties of fish, including squid and shellfish. Use whatever is available to give a good mix.

Cut the red mullet fillets into thirds. Cut the monkfish into similar-sized pieces, cutting the flesh away from the tailbone (this can be used to make stock). Cut the squid into thick rings and retain the tentacles.

Heat the oil in a large saucepan, add the onion, garlic and fennel and cook over a medium heat, stirring frequently, for 4–5 minutes until starting to soften. Pour in the wine, stir well and leave to bubble until almost evaporated. Add the tomatoes and bring to the boil, then reduce the heat and simmer, uncovered, for a further 10–15 minutes until the fennel is tender and the sauce is reduced and thickened.

Meanwhile, bring the stock to the boil in a separate large saucepan, add the mussels and cook, covered, over a high heat for 3–4 minutes, shaking the saucepan occasionally, until the mussels have opened. Discard any mussels that remain closed. Sieve the mussels, reserving the stock. Remove half the mussels from their shells, discarding the shells. Keep all the mussels warm.

Add the reserved stock to the tomato mixture and bring to the boil. Add the mullet, monkfish, squid and prawns to the saucepan and cook for 2–3 minutes until tender and the prawns have turned pink. Add the shelled and unshelled mussels and heat through. Season to taste with salt and pepper.

Transfer the stew to individual warmed soup dishes, making sure that the seafood is evenly divided. Serve each dish with the toasted bread slices and sprinkle with the parsley.

Lightly battered and fried fish

Fritto misto di mare

Serves 4–6

18 large raw prawns

225 g/8 oz cleaned baby squid

6 red mullet fillets

light olive oil, for deep-frying

lemon wedges, to serve

Batter

175 g/6 oz plain flour

2 eggs

225 g/8 fl oz cold water

salt and pepper

Mixed fried fish in batter is often served as a starter or a light lunch. The batter should be very light and crisp.

To make the batter, sift the flour into a mixing bowl. Season the flour to taste with salt and pepper and make a well in the centre. Break the eggs into the well and add the water. Gradually beat the eggs and water into the flour to form a smooth batter.

Peel and devein the prawns. Cut the squid into tentacles and rings and the red mullet into small squares.

Heat the oil for deep-frying in a deep-fat fryer, or deep, heavy-based saucepan using a thermometer, to 180–190°C/350–375°F, or until a cube of bread browns in 30 seconds. Dip the seafood in the batter and wipe off any excess. Add to the hot oil, in small batches, and cook for 2–3 minutes until crisp and golden. Remove with a slotted spoon, drain on kitchen paper and keep warm while you cook the remaining seafood.

Pile onto hot plates, season to taste with salt and serve with lemon wedges.

Grilled T-bone steak

Bistecca alla fiorentina

Serves 2

1 large T-bone steak, about
750–800 g/1 lb 10 oz–1 lb 12 oz

extra-virgin olive oil

salt and pepper

mixed salad leaves, to serve

Tuscan beef is famous, particularly the *Chianina* from the Val de Chiani. To ensure a well-flavoured steak, buy meat from a good butcher. Such a delicious treat is often eaten alone, but a simple salad of mixed leaves makes an ideal accompaniment.

Remove the steak from the refrigerator 30 minutes before cooking to return to room temperature.

Light a charcoal barbecue well in advance and add some oak chips to the coals to add flavour. When the coals are grey and very hot, put the steak on the grill rack 10 cm/4 inches above the coals. Cook for 3–4 minutes until well charred. Turn and cook for a further 3–4 minutes until rare but not bloody. Check that it is cooked to your liking. Traditionally, this type of steak is only turned once, but you can cook a little longer on both sides if you like.

Transfer the cooked steak to a chopping board and season well with salt and pepper. Cut the fillet from the bone and the sirloin separately. Thickly slice and serve immediately on warmed plates with a good drizzle of the oil, accompanied by mixed salad leaves.

Cook's tip
If you have a gas barbecue, light and preheat it to high before starting to cook. Alternatively, the steak can be cooked under a preheated hot grill or in a preheated ridged griddle pan over a high heat on the hob.

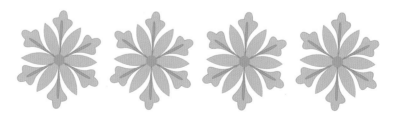

Roast pork loin

Lonzo di maiale

Serves 6

1.8 kg/4 lb flat piece pork loin, chined (backbone removed) and rind scored

3 garlic cloves, crushed

2 tbsp chopped fresh rosemary

4 sprigs fresh rosemary, plus extra to garnish

225 ml/8 fl oz dry white wine

salt and pepper

cooked seasonal vegetables, to serve (optional)

In Tuscany, whole suckling pigs are roasted in wood-fired ovens. This is a simpler recipe to enable you to cook delicious roast pork at home. Ask your butcher to keep the pork loin in one flat piece and to chine the meat and score the rind for you.

Preheat the oven to 230°C/450°F/Gas Mark 8. Put the pork loin on a work surface, skin-side down. Make small slits in the meat all over the surface. Season very well with salt and pepper (Tuscans like meat highly seasoned). Rub the garlic all over the meat surface and sprinkle with the chopped rosemary.

Roll up the loin and secure 4 rosemary sprigs on the outside with fine string. Make sure that the joint is securely tied. Season the rind with plenty of salt to give a good crackling.

Transfer the meat to a roasting tin and roast in the preheated oven for 20 minutes, or until the fat has started to run. Reduce the oven temperature to 190°C/375°F/Gas Mark 5 and pour half the wine over the meat. Roast for a further 1 hour 40 minutes, basting occasionally with the pan juices.

Remove the meat from the oven and leave to rest in a warm place for 15 minutes before carving. Remove the string and rosemary before cutting into thick slices.

Pour off all but 1 tablespoon of the fat from the roasting tin. Add the remaining wine to the juices in the tin and bring to the boil, scraping up and stirring in any residue from the base of the tin. Spoon over the meat and serve immediately with fresh vegetables, if using, and garnished with extra sprigs of rosemary.

Beef braised in red wine

Stracotto di manzo

Serves 6

3 tbsp olive oil

2 onions, finely sliced

2 garlic cloves, chopped

1 kg/2 lb 4 oz stewing steak, cut into thick strips

2 tbsp plain flour

300 ml/10 fl oz good-quality red wine, such as Chianti

2 fresh sage sprigs

200 ml/7 fl oz beef or vegetable stock

1 tbsp tomato purée

salt and pepper

1 tbsp finely chopped fresh flat-leaf parsley, to garnish

cooked seasonal green vegetables, to serve

Sometimes less-tender cuts of meat are braised in Tuscan cooking, quite often on the hob. But here the beef is cooked in the oven so that it needs little attention.

Preheat the oven to 150°C/300°F/Gas Mark 2. Heat 1 tablespoon of the oil in a large frying pan, add the onions and garlic and cook over a medium heat, stirring frequently, for 6–8 minutes until softened and browned. Remove with a slotted spoon and transfer to a casserole.

Heat the remaining oil in the frying pan, add the steak strips and cook over a high heat, stirring, for 3–4 minutes until browned all over. Sprinkle in the flour and stir well to prevent lumps. Season well with salt and pepper. Reduce the heat to medium, pour in the wine, stirring constantly, and bring to the boil, continuing to stir constantly.

Carefully turn the contents of the frying pan into the casserole. Add the sage, stock and tomato purée, cover and cook in the centre of the preheated oven for 2½–3 hours.

Remove from the oven, discard the sage and taste and adjust the seasoning if necessary. Serve immediately, scattered with the parsley, with some seasonal green vegetables.

Cook's tip

A lamb casserole can be made in the same way. Use lean leg of lamb or shoulder.

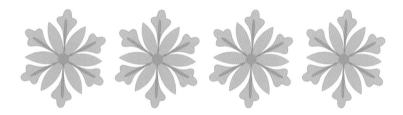

Marinated and grilled leg of lamb

Agnello al rosmarino

Serves 6–8

1 leg of lamb, about 2.25 kg/5 lb

4 garlic cloves, crushed

2 tbsp finely chopped fresh rosemary

finely grated rind and juice of 2 lemons

3 tbsp olive oil

salt and pepper

To serve

green salad

boiled new potatoes (optional)

Tuscan spring lamb is cooked very simply, as it has such a good flavour and texture. Ask the butcher to 'butterfly' it (remove the bone) for you.

Trim any excess fat from the lamb and make small, deep slits in the meat all over the surface. Transfer to a shallow dish and rub all over with the garlic, rosemary and lemon rind. Pour over the oil and lemon juice and season well with salt and pepper. Cover and leave to marinate in the refrigerator, or preferably in a larder or other cool place, for at least 4 hours, or overnight if possible, turning the meat occasionally.

Preheat the grill, or light a gas barbecue and preheat to high or light a charcoal barbecue and leave to burn until the coals are grey and very hot. Remove the meat from the marinade and pat dry with kitchen paper. Season again with salt and pepper and put on the grill rack. Cook for 2 minutes on both sides until sealed, then reduce the heat to medium–high or lift away from the coals and cook for a further 8 minutes on both sides. Test to see if it is cooked to your taste – it should be charred on the outside but still rare in the centre.

Remove from the heat, cover with foil and leave to rest for 15 minutes before carving into long strips.

Serve with a green salad and some new potatoes, if you like.

Stuffed chicken breasts

Involtini di petti di pollo

Serves 4

4 skinless, boneless chicken
breasts, about 150 g/5¹/₂ oz each

4 thin slices Italian dry-cured ham

4 slices pecorino cheese

4 cooked asparagus spears,
plus extra to serve

1 tbsp plain flour

40 g/1¹/₂ oz butter

2 tbsp olive oil

150 ml/5 fl oz dry white wine

50 ml/2 fl oz chicken stock

salt and pepper

Chickens are very popular in Tuscany and many families keep their own. Breasts are quickly cooked and here they are stuffed and served with a simple wine sauce.

Put each chicken breast between 2 pieces of clingfilm or inside a polythene food bag and, using a rolling pin, gently beat out until 8 mm/³/₈ inch thick.

Season well with salt and pepper and put a slice of ham on top of each chicken breast. Top each with a slice of cheese and an asparagus spear. Roll the breasts up carefully and secure with fine string. Dust with flour and season well with salt and pepper.

Heat 30 g/1 oz of the butter with the oil in a large frying pan. Add the chicken rolls and cook over a moderate heat, turning frequently, for 15 minutes, or until cooked through, tender and golden brown. Remove the string, transfer the chicken rolls to a warmed serving dish and keep warm.

Add the wine and stock to the frying pan and bring to the boil, scraping up and stirring in any residue from the base of the frying pan. Bring to the boil and add the remaining butter. Stir well and leave to bubble until thick.

Spoon the sauce over the chicken and serve immediately, with extra warm asparagus spears.

Cook's tip
You could use Marsala instead of white wine to give a different flavour.

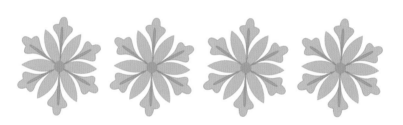

Veal escalopes with Marsala

Scaloppine al Marsala

Serves 2

4 veal escalopes, about 70 g/
2$^{1}/_{2}$ oz each

1 tbsp plain flour

3 tbsp olive oil

150 ml/5 fl oz Marsala

salt and pepper

simple risotto or green salad, to
serve

Veal escalopes can be bought ready prepared from the butcher. They are sliced from the tenderloin and then gently beaten to flatten them.

Put each veal escalope between 2 pieces of clingfilm or inside a polythene food bag and, using a rolling pin, gently beat out until 3 mm/ $^{1}/_{8}$ inch thick.

Season the escalopes well with salt and pepper and dust with the flour.

Heat the oil in a large frying pan, add the escalopes and cook over a high heat for 1 minute on each side until lightly browned. Add the Marsala and leave the liquid to bubble around the escalopes for 1 minute.

Serve immediately with the pan juices poured over the meat, accompanied by a simple risotto or a green salad.

Stuffed courgettes

Zucchini ripeni

Serves 4

4 round or long courgettes, about 115 g/4 oz each

2 tbsp olive oil

1 onion, finely chopped

2 garlic cloves, finely chopped

4 slices pancetta, diced

55 g/2 oz cherry tomatoes, chopped

2 tbsp pine kernels

4 tbsp fresh white breadcrumbs

2 tbsp shredded fresh basil leaves

55 g/2 oz pecorino cheese, freshly grated

2 tbsp olive oil

2 tbsp freshly grated Parmesan cheese

salt and pepper

Stuffed vegetables can be served as a side dish to meat or fish or as part of an antipasto. The fillings can simply be breadcrumbs and herbs or a meat filling for a more substantial meal.

Preheat the oven to 200°C/400°F/Gas Mark 6. Cut off the top of the round courgettes or cut a slice lengthways from the long courgettes. Scoop out the flesh, making sure that you don't cut through the skin, leaving a shell 5 mm/ 1/4 inch thick. Chop the vegetable flesh and put in a bowl.

Heat the oil in a large frying pan, add the onion and garlic and cook over a medium heat, stirring frequently, for 3–4 minutes until softened. Add the pancetta and cook, stirring, for 2–3 minutes until golden. Add the chopped vegetable flesh and cook, stirring frequently, for 3–4 minutes until the flesh is cooked and the liquid has evaporated.

Add the tomatoes, pine kernels, breadcrumbs, basil and pecorino cheese to the vegetable mixture, mix well and season to taste with salt and pepper. Spoon the mixture into the prepared vegetables and drizzle with the oil.

Arrange the vegetables in an ovenproof dish, cover with foil and bake in the preheated oven for 30–35 minutes until the vegetables are tender. Remove the foil, sprinkle over the Parmesan cheese and bake for a further 10–15 minutes until the cheese is lightly browned. Serve warm.

Variation

Instead of the courgettes, use 2 aubergines, about 250 g/8 oz each. Prepare and cook them in the same way as the courgettes.

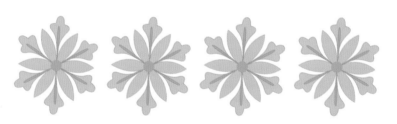

Potato and fennel bake

Patate e finocchio al forno

Serves 6

1 kg/2 lb 4 oz potatoes

2–3 fennel bulbs

4 tbsp olive oil

1 onion, finely chopped

2 garlic cloves, crushed

4 fresh sage leaves

150 ml/5 fl oz dry white wine

salt and pepper

Potatoes and fennel are both popular vegetables in Tuscany, and this dish combines them well. Use to accompany grilled meat or fish, or serve on its own as a light lunch.

Preheat the oven to 200°C/400°F/Gas Mark 6. Peel, then finely slice the potatoes. Trim, then finely slice the fennel.

Oil a large gratin dish with half the oil. Layer half the potato slices in the base of the prepared dish and season well with salt and pepper. Scatter over half the onion and garlic and cover with the fennel. Scatter the remaining onion and garlic over and season to taste again with salt and pepper. Tuck the sage leaves into the vegetables. Finish with a neat layer of the potato slices and season to taste again with salt and pepper.

Pour over the wine and drizzle over the remaining oil. Cover the dish with foil and bake in the preheated oven for 30 minutes.

Remove the foil and bake for a further 20–30 minutes until the potatoes are brown and crisp.

Cook's tip

You can use a food processor fitted with a slicer attachment for slicing the potatoes, but a mandolin is the ideal tool to use.

Desserts

Sugar was first imported into Europe from the East through the port of Venice in the Middle Ages, so it is not surprising that northern Italians have a sweet tooth. The tradition of fine pastry cooks started in those times, as feasts were prepared for the rich families of Tuscany.

As in other aspects of Tuscan cooking, local produce is important in desserts. Almonds made into biscotti are traditionally served with the local sweet wine, Vin Santo, into which they are dipped. But for a really indulgent treat, nothing can beat the rich and creamy panna cotta or tiramisù – except, possibly, the recipe here for a truly sinful soft chocolate fondant cake.

Stuffed peaches with amaretto

Peche ripiene

Serves 4

55 g/2 oz butter

4 peaches

2 tbsp soft light brown sugar

55 g/2 oz amaretti biscuits or macaroons, crushed

2 tbsp amaretto

125 ml/4 fl oz single cream, to serve

Peaches are delicious when fully ripe, simply sliced and served in some sweet white wine. But when they are not quite so ripe, this is a good alternative.

Preheat the oven to 180°C/350°F/Gas Mark 4. Grease a 20-cm/8-inch gratin dish, or a baking dish large enough to hold 8 peach halves in a single layer, with 15 g/½ oz of the butter. Halve the peaches and remove and discard the stones. If you like, you can skin the peaches by adding to a heatproof bowl of boiling water for 10–15 seconds, then transfer with a slotted spoon to a bowl of cold water. When cool enough to handle, peel away the skins.

Beat the remaining butter and sugar together in a bowl until creamy, add the biscuit crumbs and mix well.

Arrange the peach halves, cut-side up, in the prepared baking dish, and fill the stone cavities with the biscuit mixture. Bake in the centre of the preheated oven for 20–25 minutes, or until the peaches are tender.

Pour over the amaretto and serve hot with the cream.

Cook's tip
Apricots can be cooked in the same way when in season – bake in the oven for 10–15 minutes.

Poached pears in Marsala

Pere con Marsala

Serves 4

4 firm dessert pears,
such as Comice

55 g/2 oz caster sugar

2 cinnamon sticks

125 ml/4 fl oz Marsala

125 ml/4 fl oz crème fraîche,
to serve

Pears are a popular fruit in Tuscan cooking and are frequently served as part of a salad, often with walnuts and cheese. Here they are poached until tender in Marsala.

Carefully peel the pears. Cut a slice from the base of each pear and discard, then remove and discard the core from each base with a pointed knife.

Put the prepared pears in a saucepan and add enough water to just cover and the sugar and cinnamon sticks. Slowly bring to the boil over a low heat, stirring until the sugar has dissolved.

Cover and simmer gently until the pears are tender. This will take from 20–40 minutes, depending on their firmness.

Remove from the heat. Remove the pears with a slotted spoon and transfer to a serving dish. Remove the cinnamon sticks.

Return the saucepan to the heat and leave the liquid to bubble for 2–3 minutes until thickened. Stir in the Marsala and pour over the pears.

Serve warm or cover and chill in the refrigerator before serving with crème fraîche.

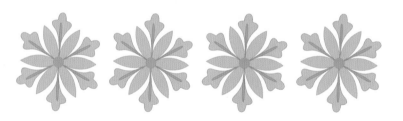

Soft chocolate cake

Torta al cioccolato

Serves 6–8

280 g/10 oz plain chocolate with at least 72% cocoa solids, broken into pieces

140 g/5 oz unsalted butter, plus extra for greasing

4 eggs, separated

55 g/2 oz caster sugar

25 g/1 oz plain flour

1 tsp vanilla extract

cocoa powder, for dusting

This is a deliciously soft, dark chocolate cake for serving as a dessert. It is like a chocolate fondant, with a velvety smooth centre.

Preheat the oven to 180°C/350°F/Gas Mark 4. Grease and base-line a 20-cm/8-inch springform cake tin with a removable base.

Put the chocolate and butter in a heatproof bowl, set the bowl over a saucepan of barely simmering water and heat until melted. Remove the bowl from the heat and leave to cool for 5 minutes.

Whisk the eggs yolks and sugar together in a mixing bowl with a hand-held electric whisk or hand whisk until thick and creamy. In a separate mixing bowl, whisk the egg whites until thick and glossy.

Fold the egg yolk mixture into the melted chocolate. Sift in the flour and fold in together with the vanilla extract. Gently fold in the beaten egg whites.

Turn the mixture into the prepared tin and bake in the preheated oven for 15–20 minutes. Do not overcook. The top should be firm but the centre still slightly gooey. Remove from the oven and leave to cool, covered, overnight.

Remove the cake tin and peel away the lining paper from the base. Dust the surface of the cake with cocoa powder and serve in slices.

Almond biscuits

Biscotti/Contucci

Makes 20–30

250 g/9 oz whole blanched almonds

200 g/7 oz plain flour, plus 1 tbsp for dusting

175 g/6 oz caster sugar, plus 1 tbsp for sprinkling

1 tsp baking powder

½ tsp ground cinnamon

2 eggs

2 tsp vanilla extract

Biscotti get their name from the Italian for 'twice cooked'. The dough is first baked in a log, then cut into slices and baked again.

Preheat the oven to 180°C/350°F/Gas Mark 4. Line 2 baking sheets with baking paper.

Very roughly chop the almonds, leaving some whole. Mix the flour, sugar, baking powder and cinnamon together in a mixing bowl. Stir in all the almonds.

Beat the eggs with the vanilla extract in a small bowl, then add to the flour mixture and mix together to form a firm dough.

Turn the dough out onto a lightly floured work surface and knead lightly. Divide the dough in half and shape each piece into a long, thick log, roughly 5 cm/2 inches wide. Transfer to the prepared baking sheets, sprinkle with sugar and bake in the preheated oven for 20–25 minutes until brown and firm.

Remove from the oven and leave to cool for a few minutes, then transfer the logs to a chopping board and cut into 1-cm/½-inch slices. Meanwhile, reduce the oven temperature to 160°C/325°F/Gas Mark 3.

Arrange the biscotti slices, cut-sides down, on the baking sheets. Bake in the oven for 15–20 minutes until dry and crisp. Remove from the oven and leave to cool on a wire rack. Store in an airtight container to keep crisp.

Cream dessert with pistachio nuts

Pistachio panna cotta

Serves 6

vegetable oil, for oiling
600 ml/1 pint double cream
1 tsp vanilla extract
4 tbsp caster sugar
2 gelatine leaves
50 g/1¾ oz shelled pistachio nuts
fresh whole raspberries or sliced strawberries, to serve

The cooked cream in this recipe makes it a rich dessert. Here, the addition of chopped pistachio nuts gives a delicious flavour and delicate colour to the dessert.

Oil 6 x 125 ml/4 fl oz dariole moulds or ramekins.

Pour the cream into a saucepan, add the vanilla extract and sugar and stir well. Bring slowly to simmering point over a low heat and simmer gently for 2–3 minutes. Remove from the heat and set aside.

Soak the gelatine leaves in a bowl of cold water for 5 minutes, or until softened. Remove from the water and stir into the hot cream mixture until dissolved.

Process the pistachio nuts in a food processor or grinder until finely ground, or finely chop with a knife. Reserve some of the ground or chopped nuts for the decoration and add the remainder to the cream mixture. Leave to infuse for 15 minutes, then sieve the mixture into a jug. Pour the mixture into the prepared moulds, cover and chill for 3 hours, or overnight until set.

To serve, dip the moulds in hot water for 2 seconds and turn out onto serving plates. Serve with a small portion of raspberries or sliced strawberries and decorated with the reserved ground pistachio nuts.

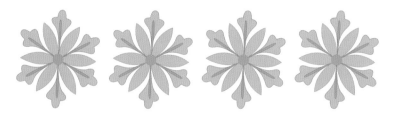

White tiramisù with strawberries

Tiramisù bianco con fragoli

Serves 6

2 eggs, separated

85 g/3 oz icing sugar, sifted

350 g/12 oz mascarpone cheese

6 tbsp full-fat milk

125 ml/4 fl oz Marsala

20 Savoiardi finger sponge biscuits

55 g/2 oz almonds, chopped

55 g/2 oz white chocolate, coarsely grated

fresh strawberries, halved, to serve

Tiramisù translates into English as 'pick-me-up'. It is a rich dessert made using mascarpone cheese mixed with eggs and usually flavoured with coffee. This is a delectable alternative.

Whisk the egg yolks with the sugar in a mixing bowl with a hand-held electric whisk or hand whisk until thick and creamy. Add the mascarpone cheese and whisk into the egg yolk mixture.

Whisk the egg whites in a separate mixing bowl and then fold into the mascarpone mixture.

Pour the milk into a shallow dish and add the Marsala. Dip the biscuits into the milk mixture just long enough to soften, then arrange half the dipped biscuits in the base of a glass or china dish about 23–25 cm/9–10 inches in diameter. Sprinkle over half the almonds. Spread over a third of the mascarpone mixture and top with a layer of the remaining dipped biscuits and the remaining nuts. Spoon the remaining mascarpone mixture over the top and swirl to give an attractive appearance.

Cover with clingfilm and chill in the refrigerator for 2–3 hours.

To serve, remove from the refrigerator and decorate with the white chocolate and halved strawberries.

Cook's tip
For a decorative effect, shave the chocolate from the block with a vegetable peeler to create chocolate curls.

Chocolate and nut cake from Siena

Panforte di Siena

Panforte is famous all over Italy, but originates from Siena. Although the recipe varies, it always contains nuts and candied peel. The addition of chocolate is often made when the cake is served at Christmas time.

Makes 1 cake

175 g/6 fl oz runny honey

140 g/5 oz caster sugar

115 g/4 oz candied lemon peel, finely chopped

115 g/4 oz candied orange peel, finely chopped

100 g/3½ oz ground almonds

100 g/3½ oz whole blanched almonds, roughly chopped

100 g/3½ oz whole blanched hazelnuts, roughly chopped

55 g/2 oz plain flour

2 tbsp cocoa powder

1 tsp ground cinnamon

½ tsp ground cloves

a good grating of nutmeg

icing sugar, for dusting

Preheat the oven to 160°C/325°F/Gas Mark 3. Oil and base-line a 20-cm/8-inch round shallow cake tin with a removable base.

Put the honey and sugar in a small saucepan and heat over a low heat, stirring, until the sugar has dissolved.

Put the candied peel in a large mixing bowl and add the nuts. Sift in the flour and cocoa powder and add all the spices. Mix well together. Pour the honey and sugar mixture over the dry ingredients and mix thoroughly together.

Turn the mixture into the prepared tin and press down well so that the surface is smooth. Bake in the preheated oven for 30–40 minutes until firm.

Remove from the oven and leave to cool completely in the tin before removing. Dust heavily with icing sugar before serving in slices. The cake will keep in an airtight container or wrapped in clingfilm and foil for up to 2–3 months.

Apricot ice cream

Gelato di albicocche

Serves 6

500 g/1 lb 2 oz ripe apricots
300 ml/10 fl oz single cream
175 g/6 oz caster sugar
200 ml/7 fl oz full-fat milk
1/2 tsp vanilla extract

A delicious ice cream that is very simple to make. Make sure that you use the ripest apricots when they are in season and at their best.

Halve the apricots and remove and discard the stones. Put the apricots in a food processor or blender and process until smooth.

Whip the cream and sugar together in a mixing bowl using a hand-held electric whisk or a hand whisk until the sugar has dissolved. Whisk in the apricot purée, milk and vanilla extract. Pour into a lidded freezerproof container, cover and freeze for 1 hour.

Remove from the freezer and whisk thoroughly using a hand-held electric whisk or a hand whisk. Re-cover and freeze for a further hour. Repeat the whisking and freezing process until the mixture is almost frozen solid. Whisk a final time, re-cover and return to the freezer until required.

Transfer the ice cream to the refrigerator 15 minutes before serving to soften slightly.

Raspberry water ice

Granita al lamponi

Granita is a frozen water ice that has large ice crystals, giving it a crunchy texture. It is easier to make at home than sorbet.

Serves 6

1 lemon
900 g/2 lb raspberries
225 g/8 oz caster sugar
150 ml/5 fl oz Vin Santo

Finely grate the rind from the lemon into a large jug. Halve the lemon and squeeze out the juice into the jug.

Put half the raspberries with half the sugar in a food processor and pulse until puréed. Pour the purée into a bowl. Repeat with the remaining raspberries and sugar. Add the Vin Santo and stir well.

Pour the mixture into a metal ice tray if available, as the metal will help to freeze the purée more quickly. Otherwise, use a lidded freezerproof container, cover and freeze for 30 minutes.

Remove from the freezer, scrape the set mixture from around the edges using a fork and fork over the mixture. Re-cover and freeze for a further 30 minutes. Repeat the mashing and freezing process every 30 minutes until the mixture is very firm.

Serve immediately straight from the freezer, spooned into chilled bowls. Granita will dissolve quickly once it starts to thaw. It is best served on the day of making, but it will keep, covered, in the freezer for 2–3 days.

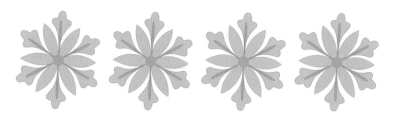

Deep-fried pastry ribbons

Cenci

Serves 8

280 g/10 oz plain flour, plus extra for dusting

2 eggs, beaten

2 tbsp light olive oil

2 tbsp caster sugar

2 tbsp Vin Santo

finely grated rind of 1 lemon

4 oranges

light olive oil or sunflower oil, for deep-frying

icing sugar, for dusting

These are crisp little biscuits made by deep-frying strips of pastry that have been cut and tied into ribbons. They are best served hot and are delicious with cold orange segments.

Sift the flour into a large mixing bowl and make a well in the centre. Add the eggs, the 2 tablespoons of oil, sugar, Vin Santo and lemon rind. Mix together with a round-bladed knife to form a dough. Use your hands to knead until smooth. Form into a ball, wrap in clingfilm and chill in the refrigerator for 1 hour.

Meanwhile, working over a bowl to catch the juice, peel and segment the oranges with a sharp knife. Add the segments to the juice, cover and chill in the refrigerator until required.

Divide the pastry in half and roll out one half on a lightly floured work surface to a rectangle about 3 mm/1/8 inch thick. Cover and repeat with the remaining pastry. Using a fluted pastry cutting wheel, cut the pastry into 10-cm x 2.5-cm/4-inch x 1-inch ribbons. Tie a single knot in each pastry strip. Alternatively, for an easier method, cut the pastry into diamond shapes and leave flat.

Heat the oil for deep-frying in a deep-fat fryer, or deep, heavy-based saucepan and using a thermometer, to 180–190°C/350–375°F, or until a cube of bread browns in 30 seconds. Add the pastry ribbons, in small batches, and cook until golden brown. Remove with a slotted spoon, drain on kitchen paper and keep warm while you cook the remaining pastry ribbons.

Dust with icing sugar before serving warm with the orange segments.

Index